The
Backwaters
Press

THE BACKWATERS PRIZE IN POETRY

"*Wolves in Shells* by Kimberly Ann Priest is a piercing rebuke of 'our dependency on machinery that harms us.' That machinery is patriarchy, marriage, and gender inequality. A blistering chronicle of a life lost—children, home, health—and regained. Muriel Rukeyser asked, 'What would happen if one woman told the truth about her life? The world would split open.' Each of these poems moves with the honesty of an ax."

—TOMÁS Q. MORÍN, author of *Let Me Count the Ways: A Memoir*

"In the first poem, Kimberly Ann Priest evokes a moment of 'dismantled vigilance—nothing encroaching, nothing to hunt,' and this becomes the quest of these stunning poems as the speaker moves through the effects of abuse and homelessness into a world free of predation. The voice in this book is strong, astute, and vulnerable as the poet reclaims her history and its fragmented beauty alongside the story of a wolf, her totem creature. Priest writes with a keen eye and great musical dexterity, creating a book that is both compelling and crucial."

—BETSY SHOLL, Maine poet laureate emeritus and
    author of *As If a Song Could Save You*

"Of wolves and shells, holy howls and spirals, does Kimberly Ann Priest weave her sacred tapestry of lyrical outpouring; in one poem she writes, 'Because I feel like thunder often, dance like snow; because I am living.' And her poems are so fiercely alive and soaring and plunging on the page that it both hurts and fills one up to read them. Hers is a startling new voice in American poetry that can never be forgotten."

—ROBERT VIVIAN, author of *All I Feel Is Rivers*

"*Wolves in Shells* is a powerful collection that details what it means to be a woman in the twenty-first century. In it, Kimberly Ann Priest documents a life of resilience after homelessness, abuse, intergenerational trauma, and witnessing the violence of America. Drawing from her cross-country travels and emotional connections to wildlife—particularly the wolves of Yellowstone National Park— Priest illustrates, in captivating detail, the strength of an individual woman who is both hunted and too often harmed but who ultimately 'become[s] her own pack' to 'survive.'"

—SUNNI BROWN WILKINSON, author of *Rodeo*,
    winner of the 2024 Donald Justice Poetry Prize

wolves in shells

Kimberly Ann Priest

The Backwaters Press
An imprint of the University of Nebraska Press

Excerpt from Johann Wolfgang von Goethe, "The Hunter's Song at Nightfall," from *Sappho to Valéry: Poems in Translation, Revised and Enlarged Edition*, translated by John Frederick Nims, copyright © 1990 by John Frederick Nims. Reprinted with the permission of The Permissions Company, LLC on behalf of the University of Arkansas Press, uapress.com.

Paw print by Christian Pietzsch, via Wikimedia Commons.

For customers in the EU with safety/GPSR concerns, contact:
gpsr@mare-nostrum.co.uk
Mare Nostrum Group BV
Mauritskade 21D
1091 GC Amsterdam
The Netherlands

Library of Congress Control Number: 2025005770

Designed and set in Garamond Premier Pro by L. Welch.

for my daughter, Ryley Eden,
&
for Charley

Contents

wolves in shells

The Howl

—of O-Six and her pups

You can almost touch the music
that spins open-aired, lungful,
unforced and willful from a pup
taught to revere a little sun
on the throat, a little meat
already in the stomach,
and momma nearby. A moment
of dismantled vigilance—nothing
encroaching, nothing to hunt.
One gray babe after another
uncertain about that first yelp,
usually a signal for danger, but then
her body stretched out on a thick
patch of grass; wrinkles forming
at the sides of her eyes from age
and survival, relaxed; and the way
the howl lingers on and on,
note by note, into that big blue
Yellowstone sky. From Slough
Creek to Lamar Canyon,
they had won themselves a place
to roam within natural boundaries
and now, this. Home
is something to fight for until
it's predator-free. I wish this for
my daughter—leisure, the earnest
present moment—as she lies
silent beside me on a beach along
Lake Michigan in sand dappled
with American dune grass.
Kingdom: *Plantae*, Family: *Poaceae*,
Genus: *Leymus*, Species: *Leymus mollis*

One hardly knows which side to take in this dramatic incident of hunger. I have tried to be impartial. I don't like wolves.

—GASTON BACHELARD

Says the Mollusk

I don't want to go home—
not forever,

but still
I want to feel
that spiraling sound
in my body

when you touch me

I Wanted to Be a Boy

because I want to be a wolf; because the earth smells
   of sinew and green. Because his hair was made of corn dust
and cloud, and I wanted to weave it around me, trust
   his sky. Because Eros did not strike my thigh or breast;
instead he plunged knives into my chest and kept the heart
   beating. Because *lunge* is so similar to *lung*, both
attempting a breath. Because I was breathing
   when my mother bore me, and this was written down
on a chart next to the names of other living things—
   and some of them were masculine; because this was not
a female breath. Because it took years to tame my teeth,
   and still I try to use them; because they are pretty. Because
I feel like thunder often, dance like snow; because
   I am living. Because his arms were made of roots,
and I wanted to trust cultivation. Because the sky tastes
   of lilac and honey; because I am breathing because its wound
has made more room inside my chest. Because I lunged
   when hungry and almost used my teeth; because
a body seems heavier after it's dead, even though it isn't.
   You can heft its corpse anywhere without cooperation
if you have the stamina. If you're big and strong enough.

When Anxious, They Tell Us to Make Our World Smaller

The strap pulled at the short hairs on my young husband's nape,
my camera slung around, as he followed me

over grassy dunes snapping photographs. I smiled,
romanced, skipped, and waved from the top of a sand heap,

then slid down like a surfer taking each rough wave
into his point and shoot, the wind

whipping up then dying, whipping up then dying—not cold yet.
He clicked and clicked until I reached the bottom,

then held the camera out for my approval, passing it softly
between us, his groomed fingertips slightly

brushing mine and his body turning to look off
into the churning waters as I lingered: right arrow, right arrow,

back, back, right arrow again—deleting some, keeping others.
Each capture, a decision, maybe all the decision

I would make in that month—something I had learned
to anticipate, isolate, frame

no matter what else he said I could not do.
Walking along the water, his bright silhouette cast itself against

a darkening sky, and I lifted the camera instinctively focusing,
taking the photo quickly then shifting to the right

as though I had always been seeking to photograph the waves:
no clear evidence we were in this scene together. The rain

came lightly but suddenly at first; he tucked
my camera under his shirt. We hurried away from the beach.

Old Shell

What drawer did you come from? What Tupperware container?
What collaged knick-knack or jewelry pendant? From what
glued photograph frame did your fragment brake off?
For what hidden arrangement did you fill a hole, that odd menagerie
of loose change, paper clips, pencil erasers, coupons, and keys
awkwardly fitted together like puzzle pieces unclaimed by their
particular puzzles? When did my daughter lose you and my
mindless hand find you tucked into the crevice of a couch or chair,
a cushion she hasn't sat on for years? What childhood
do you belong to? What memory? On what
beach of my youth did I search for you, the lone souvenir
of an afternoon hunting and watching the seagulls pick the shallows
clean of their most defenseless fish? A miniature crayfish crawls out
from underneath a rock, and there you are shimmering
next to his body. I watch how he tries to lift you with his steel blue
pinchers probably searching for his own slice
of meat. He flips you over onto your rippled back and finds
your polished belly empty, moves along, his cumbersome accordion
trailing behind him like windless unplayed keys. I pick you up,
rub your edges against my shirt, and hold you out into the afternoon
light. What preyed-upon creature once lived within you?
How close did it cling to the bone of your unarmed insides?

Wolf Story

It's the angle of the camera that makes all the difference;
everything depends on how people see. Journalists

will write the problem as too many wild mouths to feed,
all needing fresh meat, as ecologists

talk about balance with tourists gawking and smiling
from a roadside at a very safe distance, a mother and her pups

rollicking, not imagined as beasts that are ever in danger—
all that tooth and claw. From a scope,

her eyes will look hungry, pawing at scrub grass in snow
one dark winter night. It's cold, and her form

is getting gaunter. Journalists, ecologists, tourists
sleeping and the hunter protecting his cattle. My son

looks up from our board game elated by winning, the three of us
playing—mother, daughter, son—an intimate

huddle until the finale. He's searching the room for an audience:
two of us applauding, and he being *the one*.

My Mother Wears a Bikini at South Haven Beach

It's my father's favorite photograph: my mother hunched over
in a bikini, blushing. She was embarrassed, he says,

but he bought it for her and coaxed her to wear it anyway.
The photograph is fading,

bearing the orange and moss hues of an out-of-date Polaroid,
but I can still see the bright floral pattern all over

the suit. My mother's hazel eyes stare meekly up at the camera.
She was, after all, a preacher's daughter

and never as comfortable showing her cleavage as my father
was comfortable talking about sex.

Her chestnut hair falls long over her bare shoulders
framing a soft square jawline and slender ivory neck. She pulls

her left arm in to hold her right arm; her stomach is supple
but flat. Her knees are partly hidden

by water. My father is lifting
the camera, telling her to look up, please stand up straight.

Put your arms down, he says—even the lake is receding around her,
the sun as high as it can be, bathing everything in light.

A Pedagogy for Lesser Bodies

My husband kicked our dachshund puppy out the back door
because she peed a quarter-size puddle on the living room carpet.

At less than a few months old, this mishap is to be expected.
Nevertheless, he rustled her out, scooped her up with his foot

and threw her into the snow shouting profanities
that are later described to our two children as easily forgivable

frustration. They forgive him, of course, and hug him as,
through a window, I watch the puppy shiver and circle

until she finds a spot where she feels safe enough to pee.
She needs to remain outdoors, he says to the children,

to become accustomed to the cold. She needs to adjust, he explains,
a lesson she should have learned by now. He is right.

She needs to learn—and learn quickly. But she doesn't. Instead,
she becomes more nervous and pees indoors frequently.

Finally, he takes her to the vet, where she is diagnosed with bladder
malfunction, and he tells the children, so easily, that this

is a pre-existing condition, explaining we cannot afford
the medication to treat her. She is promptly shot in the head

and buried in the woods. Afterward,
he consoles our children, grieving together over her grave.

I stay in the house and watch a boiling pot of spaghetti noodles
go from stiff yellow limbs to limp white tentacles, the steam bathing

my face in faux sweat, stirring rigorously as though
this transformation demands all my attention. And, in fact, it does.

How to Do Subtraction

Take the view, for instance, from the side of the road
over mountains, hills, grass, or glade, and remember
your own, back home, through windows that seem

not breakable enough during a violent fit of rage—
no emergency exits visible, and your body already so bruised
in all the right places men can't reach with their hands;

still, you cringe under heat, balled tight. Take this away.
Take the yipping of children and dog and bury it like seeds
you've carried in pockets for years, hope, until one day

you wake hanging off the side of a bed sweating calories
you've learned not to consume to deter his comments
on how you're not thin enough, the animal

tamable to the mind overseeing the bone, and now
your arm and knee smell of exhaustion, drooping, hair matted
to the sides of your face as if you've been stalking prey

for miles for a morsel of meal to keep going. *Move on,*
he growled last night, smirking, *run away. I don't need you.*
Minus your children, you can go. *Go,* he'll say, whenever

he doesn't need you. Do the subtraction again and again
and again, with a view from a window. Slice bread,
make sandwiches. Give them all something to eat.

Taxonomy

There is a way to say a name in the present
that changes the way you say that name in its future,
like the way my own name
and my mother's name
became both blessing and curse
in the mouths of the men that spoke them.
When I first left my home
two years after divorcing my husband,
two years before my son's graduation,
and three years before my daughter wrote the poems
that would break me,
I said my daughter's name to the breeze,
then my son's name while standing by a river
in New Hampshire feeling finally free, not feeling
the names like blessing or curse,
or anything so weighty. Only
their inscription in the earth of the journey that carried me,
as if I was sure they could hear me,
as if to declare: *Mother is alive. Follow.*
As if I didn't know I was leaving.
As if I really thought they'd come running behind,
waving their arms with joy.

Elegy for Charley

who looked for me for weeks, pattered about the little house crying,
pawing at my children's legs, visibly distressed.

Who wouldn't use the bed I made in the living room; instead,
curling up in my chair, tucking his tiny terrier body into the crevice
of its arm as though I were there taking all the available space.

Who wouldn't eat much but left puddles of pee on the kitchen,
living room, and bathroom floors—drinking enough at least.

Who was swiftly given away after I left our home post-divorce
to start another life, not informed of the change
until many months had passed.

Who probably still waits for me by a back door
every day to greet me with whelps of relief and salutation,
prancing atop the faux wood planks, not stopping unless I knelt
to let his bit of tongue lick me, panting, begging.

My children said their father couldn't handle his emotions—
tears forming gobs of mucus in the corners of his eyes
as he ran about asking each inhabitant to please find me,
their father's rhetoric so convincing when he said Charley couldn't be
trusted anymore, the same words he used to frighten me away.

I was *losing control* he would whisper as a warning in my ear,
emotional at best, he would tell me;
but at worst I knew I was evidence: showing obvious signs of abuse.

Field Note on Gaston Bachelard's *The Poetics of Space*

Along the sidewalk a tiny shell—
     an omen—opens its bowled form
to my finger and thumb,
     dry and far, far away
from an ocean or lake
     as though it has traveled by air
to be lifted and homed
     inside my pocket. A talisman,
intelligible and *mysterious* [says Bachelard]
     to my hand,
its Fibonacci sequence pleasing to my eyes.
     The subjective sense
that my mother's ghost has left it
     in my path
as an anchor for *today*. The shell
     rolls inside my pocket as I flip it
over and over again,
     to worry, soothe, ponder,
and plan. To insist,
     against my own mind,
that strength is not something you muscle
     but something acquired along
the way from habits of retreat
     and resurrection. The shell
is merely a common object found
     on a sidewalk in a non-shell place, yet
I draft mythology for this
     to satisfy my need to believe
that my mother has been here all along,
     watching my life surface,

guiding as I wander and stray; this is what we do
    in every story.
I drop the shell into the ashtray in my car,
    turn the engine on.
It stutters happily inside
    its new metal cave
with each bump and turn the road takes.

Two Wolves

My son, the battle is between two wolves inside us all.
One is evil...
　　　　　　　　　　　　—The Legend of Two Wolves

He slides the card across the kitchen counter, worried.
"My wife had this," he says, as I read *anger, envy, sorrow, regret,*

and he looks at me with the same question he's repeated over
and over: "Did I do this to her?" ... *arrogance, self-pity, guilt* ...

her suicide as fresh in his mind as the information about her rapes
years ago ... *hope, serenity, humility.*

He wants me to look at her journals ... *kindness, benevolence, empathy*
... mostly to answer his questions, the card that she carried

in her pocket empowering a young boy to choose ... *truth,*
compassion. "Why would she do this to her daughters?" he asks.

I look down at the answer given in typical parable form as a question.
I can't tell him he's not responsible

since the earth, it seems, is given to men.
Whatever we feed, say the Cherokees, [whomever] is the wolf

that will win. I respond with assurance that the legend is a good one
to cherish—the edges of the card worn, dirty, and curling.

Everything's Fine

Tonight, I'll shoot the moon, put a bullet right through
its one audacious bright eye—pithy phrase by pithy phrase,
a show down, teaching my body to conceive America's lies
as if I love this gun for how it can eradicate
the broken down, hungry creature in me, hastening
God's judgment on any wild limb too lively
to consume. Daughter, I shivered
in the back of my Jeep, grateful you weren't there
to see me shivering. Fear, I've been told, is for the weak,
and I swallowed that bullet so hard so many times it almost
killed me—arms pinned down, hair flung back,
child, wife, mother, daughter, cold floors, a closet, the bed,
danger, along with ten thousand or so voices raised in prophecy
concerning my healing. America, the weapon
of our choosing as if we've all always been choosing.
America when I told you, "I'm okay girl. Everything's fine."

Open Mic

To swallow me whole, they dropped the money
into the hat and passed it around like I had done
something magic with tongue and teeth and gut.

A handful of whoops and shouts—a dozen
hallelujahs—not enough to deliver me from the pocketful
of dollars I wouldn't spend on a hotel night,

so used to saving and sleeping in my car. Flashlights
in the passenger window. Cops. *Move along now*,
they'd say, kindly. I'm a white girl. It's okay. That night,

I'd preached a mighty fine sermon of poems,
the crowd convinced, powerfully, that the violence
of a past life won't kill me. Performance

unrolling my sleeping bag, again, in the glow
of another well-lit gas station parking lot: profits
and gains, Arkansas. My soul, forever, to keep.

Steven Turnball

—of the hunter that shot O-Six

I imagine him surly, full beard and flannel,
a soft self-tanned leather coat and maybe a few bad teeth

from too much tobacco. His accent indicating
isolated living and a poor education—backwoods Wyoming

American, like the kind that value independence
over everyone else. In truth,

the author says his house was tidy right down to the polished
bone: antlers for drawer pulls, photos of kills

hung everywhere, and her pelt draped lovingly
over his arms then hung on a hook by the door

so the author could view her full beauty, gray coat
soft and thick, grown for the winter

he shot her. *I didn't do anything wrong*, he said, admiring
the animal, the receipt for his government-issued wolf tag

mounted in the other room. He was right.
She was killed outside the protections of Yellowstone

at a range that required no special skill.
I put in my time to get that wolf, he bragged to the author;

he had followed her movements for weeks, studied his prey,
paid the hunter's fee for a license—ended her life ethically.

After Leaving

What she won't be able to tell you, then,
is about the guilt as she's staring down the barrel of their gun,

exhausted. She won't say anything, just wait
for the bullet, her body a habit of lurching: forward,

forward, stop. You can ask any questions. Make any
assumptions, requests, have her wallet, coat, or mind.

Even her children. You see,
there was so much paperwork, legal paperwork,

and her life not worth enough to get beyond the paperwork,
so that, when a letter came from a lawyer

telling her she had to leave the home because her ex-in-laws
owned it, she was only a little surprised—

two years divorced, alimony ended, months
of unemployment and asking for more time. They didn't

need her anymore—money to be made
from all five properties, and they'd finish raising

her children for her, they said. So kind. Besides,
their son was doing better now—just some anger issues

and enough good guilt to cleanse him of the habit. He's got
Jesus now, they'd tell her, then, *you need to get a job.*

She didn't say anything at all. Maybe they were right,
and she could pay the rent if she got some Jesus too.

I Don't Tell My Daughter I Wrote Another Wolf Poem

If you had suffered more this would be easier.
I'd say, *Peel your carcass off that floor girl*
and give him something to pray about. But you tell me
he's good to you,
and he cries a lot. Dad,
you say, is sad, is sorry—and I believe you.
I want to anyway. No one
is all bad all the way down to the bone, right?
I mean, I wish this were not true,
that one of us was *all* bad—he
or me. I wish
the totem animal pursuing us both
into exoneration (our afterlives)
acted so much saner,
not generating all this chaotic divisibility.
But math has never been my better subject—it's too easy.
There's a place for every number to go,
some disappearing into a logical nowhere.
My animal will eat me, I know. I love him too much.
Daughter, I think he'll eat the both of us.

If we remain at the heart of the image under consideration,
we have the impression that, by staying in the motionlessness
of its shell, the creature is preparing temporal explosions,
not to say whirlwinds, of being.

—GASTON BACHELARD

The road goes east, the road goes west,
But not a road goes back.

—JOHANN WOLFGANG VON GOETHE,
"The Hunter's Song at Nightfall"

Among Fingernail Clams

—the shallows
may not be a realm
of power

but here the fettered
teem against the shoreline
considering

Protections

Against the whir of my treadmill
    a shot rings out

and a wolf is gunned down—O-Six,
    they named her,

numinous alpha female
    of Yellowstone National Park

because she survived
    solo.

Even the commentator says
    this was unusual

and dangerous; yet she was beloved
    for acuity

and beauty, face like an owl mask against
    snow white.

I listen as the hunter celebrates
    his kill, the documentary

rolling. My treadmill
    rolling.

They had lifted the ban on hunting
    wolves that year—

endangered status just long enough
    for a female

to become her own pack, survive, surpass
    the males of her kind.

At the Eli and Edythe Broad Art Museum

UNBUILT RESIDENCIES
lightweight wood / plaster / papier-mâché / concrete

Katrín Sigurdardóttir has unbuilt a neighborhood of homes,
transportable and set upon a platform

to be unenclosed, unadorned, unseen from the inside: glass-
less windows and torn open sides, gorgeous rafter to plaster,

bone to bone, their injuries not inflicted externally
but as part of their integrity—and where the skin is cut, edges

made raw by faux exposure to wind, rain, heat,
and below-zero temperatures. Maybe indifference, predation,

ego, and grief. Four years ago, I shed my home,
left its deadness behind and slept, like a mollusk, in my Jeep

several nights, driving toward nothing in particular
but what I hoped would be a new definition of *place*. Home-

lessness is frightening, but not nearly as much
as the constant upkeep of spaces that do not define your soul-life.

My body was tired of the walls my husband sustained for us,
so I let the elements have me. *Mollusk* is derived from the Latin word

mollis—it means *soft*. To love a home is to let it evolve
like a body, to participate, to ask it what it wants to be. Kneeling

to the height of these pained structures I search
their shells for signs of ambulant life, hear only the animal silence.

A Patch of Blue

Strapped to a gurney, I watched the sky frown and close behind me
as the ambulance pulled away from the civilized world
just hours after our new president was named. Homeless, broke,

I would never see a bill from that visit,
and I would also never have my democratic say. Now,
nearly a term later, my daughter and I sit at Denny's Diner

considering candidates as she stares into her phone reading
their values and plans. I tell her stories
about how Medicare saved me, the importance of listening,

and all the reasons not to follow the voting advice of her dad.
There are many women like me, I say, remembering the moment
the psychiatrist wrote PTSD and handed me a script for medication

to level serotonin. Mere hours earlier her father had stated,
emphatically, that this was not *his* fault, not *his* responsibility,
that the years of pounding and thrashing, screaming and threatening

were all in my head. He was right—a few scribbles on paper
to confirm this, and the gaping silence of family and friends—
my packed bag plunked down on a floor next to a hospital bed

as the skin on my legs began itching from not shaving.
This morning, I poke at the stack of pancakes swimming in syrup
as my daughter lifts her eyes in revelation: *Mom!*

I know who I'm voting for! I smile. *Yeah? Yeah*, she says. At eighteen,
she leans into me, telling me often I am the only parent
she can trust. We finish our coffee and stare out the window.

I still don't know who to vote for this primary; I only know
who *not*. She breaks my contemplation with the inevitable question
after a long explanation of Medicare-for-All

during which the clouds shallow and part, losing their possession
of this unusually warm Michigan spring day: *Who will you vote for Mom?*
The servers and cooks clink and shuffle behind us, their jocular

demeanor exposing our northern vulnerability to a little bit
of post-winter sun. I didn't see the sky outside that hospital room
for almost three days, or even realize it was happening.

Luxuries

The sticker on my dashboard is from you, Daughter,
a luxury I keep while driving out West,

home free, like I've always wanted to be.
I've howled at the full moon, I tell you, laughing,

watching my breath expire into a frozen plume.
It's cold. I miss you

and the couch I'd curl up beside for hours
while you were away for the day

at school, its gentle upholstered slope sitting up straight
and a curved leg grasped firmly

in my hand as I pulled my whole body
into a bright spot of sun on the carpet, sobbing, asking

a white man's God to save me, crying
myself to sleep and licking my paws for their pain.

On the Ishnala Trail

Solidago canadensis crown acres of woodland fields
on either side of the trail.
They stand regal in pyrimidal-shaped inflorescence,
bold mustard yellow pitched into
a cerulean sky. Secund blooms dangle
from each stem, dainty and hanging
like little bells tolling gently with each breeze
that lifts, the fields waving
yellow yellow yellow. "By itself
alone," Ishnala proclaims, a Winnebago name
given to the burial grounds nearby
where a large lone rock extends over the waters
of Mirror Lake as its symbol;
but each stalk of chiming gold is not alone.
Rather, their saint-like postures
bundle together so thick one could not easily
pass through them. They sway
and pronounce nothing but the abundance of August
and September. Together, they ripen and pray.
I am also not, today, *by myself*
alone among these flowers,
or the trees that canopy over me as the trail leads
away from the fields and into the woods.
Ishnala, I repeat over and over again,
ishnala, ishnala—a response to what my father said
when I told him I couldn't get a job
and had no permanent place to go,
and he answered, *Get married*,
and I let the phone fall away from my face,

the simplicity of his reply startling in its brief summation
of my worth or that any man
would suffice for this. *Ishnala*, I speak
to the wild world around me—plea, pardon, manifesto.
A stream dances along the trail
like a child inviting me to play;
nearby, a park bench opens, waiting to receive me.

Dad

I bet you told her right off that you were in the navy
and a college boy now, proud pack of smokes on the table
at the local Howard Johnson's, marketing genius
when you saw her in a mini-skirt, notebook in hand, approaching—
her butter-chestnut hair, warm smile, a stack of pancakes
and hot maple syrup. The coffee and the bill: only three dollars
from your worn leather wallet in the square front pocket
of a corded jacket, Sherpa collar. You gave up the cigarettes
quickly after you married for three meals a day and three children
to raise, but Momma smoked her first—post having me—
in the Lansing apartment and her last when you caught her
and crushed the whole pack. There's always something in you
fighting for your rightness after you've finished exploring
your own wrongness. *I didn't marry a smoker*, you once told me—
but you *did* marry Momma because she had good legs.

For Practical Purposes

Sometimes you land in a wasteland, the sun
bright over wheat-colored grass waving in all directions
lorded by wind. Here,

I watch the fields praise the sky and learn a little
about love from the local churchgoers,
even though I promised myself I'd never do religion again.

We all vote conservative, the preacher's wife says,
sipping her coffee on a couch
at the local coffee shop where the people are hospitable

and the sign on a bookshelf reads, unashamedly,
Jesus is King. I plan to stay here only as long as I have to,
borrowing the couch of a friend and clinging

to my daughter over the phone. I tell her, maybe,
a little faith won't hurt us—a stipend of belief might help
keep us strong. After all, I say,

God is not voting for anything other than our hearts.
She listens to me reconsider *God*, knowing my choices
are limited and that,

in every location, while homeless, I must trust someone.
Here in Oklahoma, *Jesus*.
The locals say I can take him everywhere I go.

Because Memory, I Am Told, Is Unreliable—

Lie, just a little, about the color of the grass, the quality of sky,
the air and whether it is breathable. For instance

that house across the street is not broken down yet,
its sockets retaining the same panes of glass it was born with

just like the eyes we keep forever if we can—aging,
but the same. Tell me it isn't February and colder

than usual. Don't explain to my soul beauty;
I don't want to know. I want to believe that this small town

is a place I'd stay forever. That the men
smoking outside of the halfway house don't scare me much—

or intrigue me some because I am also *halfway.*
That after years of being named the offender by my abuser

[the man from whom I'm still running], I'm not confused
concerning the snow falling today and whether

it is desirable for its whiteness and coolness on my face,
or if I am tired of its falling. I only know how long

I've been tumbling into grief and too many questions—
a disassociation from every present moment into an obscure past.

The house across the street invites workers for remodeling;
the coffee shop in town makes breakfast sandwiches I like.

Irregular Patterns of Endangered Migrations

He is pine needle and shell—long brown hair, chiseled shoulders,
a merman in a landscape fluid, always forested

and moving like something breathing underwater. We climb,
loot-logged, as my guide helps me obtain solid footing

on the next rock along the trail we take to the summit
of Tumbledown, a small mountain in Maine, and the way he stays

close enough to steady me at a moment's notice
is like watching someone who has memorized the currents

in this elevated air. I have never seen
green so verdant, climbed terrain so rugged—never trusted a man

so quickly without suspicion of his history,
but the higher we pull our bodies toward heaven, the less

history itself seems important to the land. We stop
halfway up as he lifts my pack off my shoulders, sits down

beside me on a large stump along the trail, lets me surface, catch
my breath, muscles unconditioned for climbing.

He has lived near this mountain since he was a child, and
at the top, he says, there is a lake clear as a mirror

where reality itself seems unlawfully suspended. I had known him
only a few hours when I asked him to *please take me there.*

Mountain Story

The Grand Hogback mountains stretch north to south for miles,
mere fossils of what they used to be, from McClure Pass
to Meeker, Colorado. In Canon City,

hikers take the road that winds to the top to watch the sun set
to the west right over the small, isolated valley
surrounded by prisons and residence to inmate families. Homeless

for months now, I'm staying with a friend in a house too small
for she, her husband, their toddler, and grandmother. While here,
I drive the windy roads through the Hogbacks

exploring little towns and beautiful countryside to keep
out of their way. The sun sets late in early October,
burnishing the bright yellow leaves of aspen trees so that they look

like yield signs against the gray-blue landscape,
making it difficult to reconcile the contrast of underground prison,
barbed wire, and grid-like halogen lights tucked into rural folds.

This evening, I sit on a smooth surface at the top of a small mountain
along the road that winds, one-way, up and down the other side.
Cars line the road; hikers line the peak,

collectively reverent as shadows grow longer and the western horizon
is outlined in resplendent white light, canyon ridges
crowned sharp and majestic for the minutes the sun lingers

just behind. I could sit here gazing forever, grasping
for nothing more than uninterrupted time, the way a caged bird
must feel when dawn first glows through an eastern-facing window,

reaching beyond the glass with his light-eliciting song because, surely,
this is a portal, and he is now part of a chorus of birds
in the wild yard unfolding its green invitation. The sun

dips so low that hikers start descending, cars slowly inching their way
down with headlights on to give everyone a little more light.
But I'm lost in the beauty around me—

as is the middle-aged man sitting in his unpainted SUV.
He stares at me with morbid attention, hat pulled low over his eyes,
unaware that I perceive his intentions. Suddenly cognizant,

I notice that other hikers have nearly made it to the bottom
of this tiny mountain, so I flip out my phone and pretend
to talk to a friend as I start down the road, the SUV

slinking slowly behind me. Then, spinning around to face him,
I smile and walk past, nodding cheerfully and stupidly.
He keeps descending, going the right way on this one-way repeat.

Field Note on Gaston Bachelard's *The Poetics of Space*

Maybe it was the face,
    or the nest of seaweed beneath
the laser-cut conch shell,
    or the fact that I wasn't sure
if it was worth even five dollars
    to slip the pendant onto one of
my trusty pewter chains
    and wear it around my neck.
For whatever reason,
    I didn't buy it at the local artist's market
even though it caught my eye.
    I picked it up
with half a notion to hold the flat coin
    against my ear
and listen for its ocean, the coin's face
    peering, expressionless, off into
a distant nowhere to my right; she
    inside the conch.
She encased in its trumpet:
    an instrument fashioned
to amplify sound
    weighing less than an ounce
in the palm of my hand—a woman
    groomed her whole life to fit onto
its one-dimensional plane.
    Holding the coin, considering,
running my thumb over its surface,
    I lingered so long that the market attendant
asked me if I'd found something
    I liked. I had: outside,

afternoon light warmed the crisp air of late
    autumn, leaves fallen to the sidewalk
and dried. Venders busy
    with heat lamps and Saturday.

The Unusual Art of Living Well

Olivia smiles out at blue-gray water, miles of driftwood and stone
thrown up against the shore. She is oyster in homemade hat,

cold nipping at the soft parts of her face. Presque Isle
frames itself nicely in her phone's camera—photographs she sells

to make a meager living on the internet. There,
pink flamingos dance beak-to-wing-to-toe in silver shallows,

a *Sarasota Salsa*, alongside three tall posing palms titled *Stooges*,
their fronds personalizing each dowdy head. Boats moor *Haven Island*

in a sea of red, white, and green paint along its coast, their little ropes
reaching toward a viewer. And in Mexico,

she has summoned a series of *Jalisco Ghosts*—swirling folk dancers
implied by widespread blurred rainbows, tanned heads, hands,

and leather-heeled feet. A city arcs into bright cobalt
blue, and she calls it simply *St. Louis*; not like *Yard Flowers in Cleveland*

or *Grungy Pittsburgh Garages*. And she has so much to say
about Michigan, where the dunes and lakes are always beguiled

by its photo-friendly people: *Girl in Beach Hat, Boy Collecting Shells*,
and *Swimmers at Ludington Lighthouse*. Today,

her own pockets are filled with the red rocks of Lake Erie
and sea glass she scuttles from sand in hand before leaving the beach

to walk toward a van laden with all her worldly treasures. *Ohio*,
it reads in blocked metal letters, as well as Missouri,

Florida, Georgia, and Maine, stickered
for all the places she's been since a three-year divorce left her

with nothing—a husband's final revenge. Next, she says,
she will go to Nova Scotia: I can follow her there on Instagram.

How to Forgive the Predator

All living things must eat.
The stomach is not impartial; neither

the soul. We survive
by what we do and do not nurture,

and sometimes this requires teeth.
I say to my son, *Don't incise*

the soft part of your heart.
But he does,

creating a scar—each time toughening,
each time making the tissue

less susceptible to pain. When I got
divorced I learned quickly

that this is what made me desirable
for eating, having been broke down

by a mallet, my husband's
hammering anger tenderizing me.

Having forgotten pain.
Having learned not to squeal

in a cage but continue to release
the lactic acid that keeps the slaughter

from spoiling. My son
teaches himself to forget pain too

in the same house, on the same street,
with the same sort of fleshly

cravings, a little indifference
to break down his appetite for love.

After I Tell a Man I Can't Date Him
Because of My Hidden Disability

A rusted bottle cap pokes up from the sand next to three dry leaves
the color of dull lemons. The Wisconsin river
smells of freshwater fish; I am happy with my life.

Rust pink, old broccoli green, silver ripples—the colors
all around me—and the hum of traffic on a distant bridge. This place
is for motorcyclists and hangovers, like the one I'm nursing now,

unintended from only two beers last night, a night I tried to be
like all the others drinking beer and laughing,
the woman next to me rubbing her tits up against a man's chest

because they are old friends in small-town America and here,
in these friendly-sort-of rural islands,
you can do things like that without consequence.

I lie on the blanket I spread over the sand, a book beside me—always
a book, my lover of choice because I need someone understanding
in my life who will carry on a long conversation.

I read each book I love all the way through, listening,
asking questions, hoping the book will offer me something by way
of a mental orgasm and stay with me for life

because I want to believe that I'm happy. I am.
Freshwater fish stir the river lined by a rust-pink beach and trees
that look like old broccoli. This is such

a small town—the kind you try to leave when you're young to find
the guy you think you want to have. I did,
and this is the post-traumatized brain he gave me I explained to the man

at my table between beers and a few semi-honest laughs. My book
is good but not good enough to compete with this hangover,
three dry leaves the color of lemons, a rusted bottle cap.

Hunter's Moon

Outside my window, branches fold to prayers, and I wonder
 if leaving was worth it—
time pregnant and moving laboriously, searching for closure
 with the same man over and over again.
A confusion of moonlight, unsympathetic orb
 governing over my shoulder—smile here, dimple there,
glow before the harvest—reminding me I have always been
 reflecting a much grander sphere.
Ammunition counted into phone calls and texts,
 insisting I consumed my own body, carved my bones
into his landscape, and laid down to bleed. I sit
 beside the window catching magenta in a warm cup of tea,
contemplating the stockpiling I've done: bullet stings, bare
 hands, wasp whispers. My shaking.
The weather razor sharp by late November—but October,
 still a wish of green as I learn to pace myself,
my children watching leaves turn against their own windows,
 faraway lamp-lit stars
as distant tonight as the few specks I see when I look up.
 I name each fixed point for them, a stylus
replaying devotion, the unbroken habit of staying close to home
 to feel safe—waking each morning
with hope to find a note from my husband scrawled
 across my pillow: *I'm sorry for everything I do*, present tense.

Nocturne

My guide retrieves a few potatoes from a sack
and slices them into an aluminum mug,
our makeshift pan because he forgot the real one.

We have hiked into a fog
obstructing the view of the pine tops for miles
that he hoped to show me.

But I am satisfied with the view
from our tent door as he leans over the fire
patiently turning the stew,

his long curly hair pulled back from his face,
his t-shirt tight. He brings me
the stew on a plate, then returns

to the fire to cook more food
as the rain begins to come quicker, soaking through
his clothes and streaming down the back

of his neck. His face glows
with concentration while the night grows darker
around us, and around us a world is built—

whatever our minds attune it to be.
I savor my meal of chicken, potatoes, and squash,
chewing the meat slowly. Here,

the silence, the starlight,
the insignificant orb of our tent—a man's quiet
breath over a fire as he cooks a meal

of his own in hard rain.
A sharp beat of wings rustles the pine overhead—
the aggression of a lone imagination.

Gestation

... it grew in the dark body, pulsing,
and took flight with the lips and the mouth.

—Pablo Neruda

The word, says Neruda, was born in the blood. My son
watches blood drip from my mouth when I become too tired to care

anymore. He understands my hunger at only ten years old. Later,
he will tell me the light also went out of my eyes. *Mom,*

he says, *I remember*—the light in his eyes flickering again,
though ever so dimly, and "the atmosphere tremb[ling]

with the first word[s] produced [of] panic and groaning"; [yes,
Neruda, "from darkness"]. We stand in a parking lot

not hugging because, now, he is a man. Now, "syllable, flank
of long light and hard silver": a voice repeating, *if you don't like your life*

kill yourself [his father's], and silence between us to save us
from the blood of the one of us who does not outlive its producing.

America

It's a matter of opinion—the word, how we use it,
    what it means. Daughter,
you'll catch your breath so many times while searching for its *place*,
    feeling all your weight, heavy and loaded
and ready to go off inside yourself, inside your own pain.
    Because it's out there somewhere—home—
and they'll tell you you can have it
    if you add to your burden of losses *forgiveness*,
lay it upon your already expiring bones. America
    is good. It will keep you righteous, always sniffing the air
for a mouthful of meat. Incentive. Daughter,
    how can I explain this hunger to make my soul
right with God even if it kills me, simply because I'm caught
    in the bind of not enough sleep? It's not
integrity they're after, but that's what they'll tell you,
    and that's what you'll believe,
I promise. Daughter,
    I don't want you to be homeless even if it kills you
not to be—a kicking near-carcass needs every calorie
    it earns just to fight off the fleas.

Of my mother's voice—the ocean's voice—the murmur of the sea.

—E. W. BÄÄRNHIELM, "Song of the Seashell"

Borders

so much displacement—

the sand easily shifted
and swept away

miles of beach
a vast congregation
shimmering in sunlight

Unpacking

My daughter opens a box of books
and begins stacking them

in a corner one at a time, saying aloud
their names—my nerves

sway with the motion of her arms.
Unspecified depressive

disorder reads the paperwork
I pull out

of the file box,
underneath PTSD. At which I ponder

two years of intermittent
homelessness,

separation from children, loss
of partner, family, and friends. The way

the man now walking through the door
of my new apartment

with another box of books and a little lamp
abused me

for coming apart at my seams
with barking dogs

and the clank of dishes in a sink,
too much TV at 6 a.m. Sunday morning,

his mother's this and that,
all the relatives crowded into

his parents' living room space,
and me slipping away to decompress.

I open a box of bowls and cups,
begin stacking them gently

while my ex-husband
leaves to grab more boxes to unpack.

The both of us falling into the rhythm
of our marriage:

he the heavy lifter and I
the curator of all our fragile parts.

We do this in relative silence,
still not saying what needs to be said,

the unspecified truth my psychiatrist
is not trained to properly name:

this perfectly functional occasion,
the order we crave,

our dependency on machinery
that harms us.

Preacher's Daughter

Her hair, a burnt bush dyed to match
    the brittle branches of late autumn.
She shuffles in bathrobe and slippers
    slopped with egg I watched her drop,
brush carelessly away leaving
    yolk smears. She has
remarkable red lines in her aging skin,
    standing there speechless from the strokes,
my mother lipsticking her face, re-rouging
    her cheeks, licking her thumb
to pull a smudge of shadow off a lid: too thick—
    redrawn the shape of angel wings
or eagle wings, something wider than her eyes.
    She works at her image
in the mirror as though she is going somewhere,
    somewhere appearances matter:
such as the front row of the church
    Sunday morning—she,
nine years old and observing her father,
    a man double the height of the pulpit,
preaching, his eyes always favoring
    balconies and roof beams, anything
higher than the lintel of the door.
    She never talked about the bruises
and belt marks he left on her backside, ankles,
    thighs; at least, not without looking up,
the way her large brown eyes search
    the space behind her in the mirror
as though she waits for Father to come
    pin the hair back, wipe the egg off,
let her tell him how he loves.

My Daughter and I Gather Stones at Empire Beach

> *Wolves in shells are crueler than stray ones.*
> —Gaston Bachelard

I have been watching documentaries on wolves for days now.
The weather is changing, signaling the seasonal habit
of staying indoors; but today, a little sun. We leave
our coats in the car and walk out to the beach to gather cold white
stones worn smooth by innumerable rising tides and strewn
horizontally along the shoreline. The stones
are dry, leaving dark impressions in the sand where we harvest.
My daughter tells me to find a rock large enough to paint on.
I do. These days, she is a cub following, learning, memorizing
my every move, affection-starved from the few years I was away.
She holds up a perfect stone and says this is the one she will paint on,
then turns to take photos of the lake, the shore, the setting
sun hung gloriously over the water. I came back to her
like a lone wolf traveling home after a failed re-wilding. Now,
she leans into the stories I tell about the places I have been
and wants to see them too—wants both of us to leave
these shores and start again somewhere different, somewhere
that does not groan under the weight of her father's abuses.
I wish it were that easy, that this world was not his world
everywhere I go. When wolves were re-introduced to Yellowstone,
some tried to return to Canada, an arduous journey
over life-threatening terrain, because they knew it would be easier
to find shelter and food in the familiar, deal with predators,
keep their cubs safe. Stories of the wild are often one-sided
and far too heroic, told by tellers best positioned for a thrill.
I don't tell my daughter I almost drove to the ocean to build

last campfires and die. I don't tell her about homelessness, hunger,
or the men who tried to harm me. I don't tell her wolves 9 and 10
got lost in the Absarokas or that 10 was gunned down
by a white man in Red Lodge, Montana—and that he was proud
of his kill. I tell her 9 and all her pups survived.
My daughter stares out at these waters like a woman attuned
to a calling. I don't tell her that someone had to gather them
into a vehicle and bring them back to where they were protected—
I don't tell her this is why I also came home.

At the Butterfly Habitat

> *Complacency and false-positive assumptions about the resiliency*
> *of once-common species can have tragic consequences when timely*
> *action is not undertaken to safeguard their populations.*
>
> —Center for Biological Diversity

Cruz points to a stalk of milkweed and explains that this is
monarch food. We are surrounded by a former cornfield
now turned into small farm plots for refugees and food banks—

and this butterfly habitat. He cuts me a stalk and feeds it through
the mouth of a used water bottle we find in the field and fill
with well water; then he holds up a monarch caterpillar in a cup.

We have to manage them now, he says, waving a hand out at the field
that requires constant tending to keep weeds from overtaking
the newly reinstated native species. The caterpillar

munches voraciously on small leaves protruding from a small
stick in the cup. Cruz gives me the milkweed and the cup
and begins searching a tomato plant to find the large praying mantis

he located earlier as he explains that they eat both lady bugs—
a helpful species—and other bugs destructive to his struggling
native plants. *The mantis is undiscriminating*, he says,

but he lets it be and *takes one for the team*. We don't find the mantis,
so my tour culminates in an invitation to weed the land anytime
as Cruz points to and names various invasive plants that threaten

the habitat so I will know what to pull up and what not to. I use
my phone's camera to photograph the weeds—data for when I return.
But for now, I will take the caterpillar home, feed him milkweed,

watch him cocoon, then set him free full-winged. *He will do a little dance*, Cruz says, *to test the air before flying*. The whole process meticulous—man, insect, plant. I look out at the work he has done,

at what appears to be a tatty field—not the raw resources of butterfly survival—slightly pleased that I can do something for this lone would-be monarch, already sick, already dying in my cup.

First Visit to the Sister Survivors Exhibit

*The teal ribbon was chosen to represent sexual assault in July of
2000 by the National Sexual Violence Resource Center, along
with the designation that April would be the month dedicated
to honoring survivors.*

The chiffon butterflies that vine across the ceiling are delicate
as my grandmother's lips, smiling into me; her teal eyes
code themselves into every bright angle of light
that turns out to be a spotlight on a face. Wrinkled trees—
delimbed—stand like a copse of petrified saints in the corner
of the room, gauze tied at their waists, tiny like my waist
when I was a bubbly two-year-old balanced on her lap
and beaming into a camera for the photograph that now hangs
in my parents' apartment. All I remember of this woman
rushes into the present, my body seizing with realization
that she might not have died soon enough,
several months after the photograph. That she might have come
close to me after a man molested me—an event six years
in my future—and I might have, with disfigured perception,
distrusted her kindness for many years after that.
I scope the museum walls, finally settling on an inscription:
*You handed me a pin from the 2012 Olympics to ensure my silence, telling me
how special I was.* I was special, bouncing on her knee three
or four times so she could get me to smile for the camera.
She made popping and cooing noises to encourage laughter
and compliance—an ugly gesture out of context.
I suffered, reads another inscription, *but I told myself to be tough.*
Soft baby skin folds around her hands, her slender manicured
fingers circumferencing my body as she bears
her pearly white teeth at me and I bear mine—impossibly
dainty and straight—toward the camera man, he

57

and Grandmother working hard to capture my attention
and maintain a cheery expression so I will maintain mine.
A balancing act. *For years*, the inscription laments, *I had this atrocious
secret and fear. I felt so much shame and embarrassment.* I feel
the flinching in my body while standing in this room alive
as a tomb where her perfumed image materializes suddenly
and bends close to mine, teal eyes smiling, soft lips lilting into my lost
little face—hands holding out a candy for her "special" girl.

INEZ JENNIE
(OLSON)
GREIG
(1907–81)

Spirit of the Animal

at an event dedicated to
survivors of sexual assault

I have no sound for the hollow part
of my grief—my open mouth aggressively
windless, my body folded as a reed,
the force of a northerly breath too strong,
dividing my gut, cutting its current,
complicating the power of what feels so uncontainable
yet stays so contained. That long caw
of pain. Bay of wolf or hiss of cat—
the whole spirit of an animal invested
in its voice, the whole body pulling in
then pulling out, rising up, divorcing me,
walking away, it being
so disappointed with my lack of posture,
the way the wolf or cat would at least
round their shoulders, form their face.
But I am too slain, too stunned
by what I did not see coming. Like the figure
on stage, mere stem of a woman explaining
the rape—not about the rape but explaining it
as though there is some reasonable shape
to irrational deeds; as though there is
a plot line, some lesson learned, she says.
She shuffles her feet, looks down at the floor,
a rag heap of bare whispers, wind whistling over
her lips; every woman thereafter admitting
she is wiser now than she was before.
This will not happen again, they say, shoulders
slumped, shuffled feet, eyes staring at
the floor, bodies swaying back and forth—
oh, oh, oh.

Upon Viewing Katrín Sigurdardóttir's *Metamorphic*

/ craft paper / plaster / marble /

This tatty couch, that stiff chair,
the calico floor strewn with a few somethings—a child's
room. All the gray relic of our worst imaginations
set out spaciously and pattered with blocks
of soft sun pouring through gridded glass behind
and to the left—eye level. No bed. */ bland /* You could
walk right into the maze, sit down in the center,
begin playing */ reconstructing /* but for the blurred bodies
in the doorway watching. One shuffles her feet,
the other straightens her coat. Paid positions. How
to explain that, sometimes, we must get as close to a thing
as we can, crawl into the faux arrangement, lie on
the couch, sit in the chair, pretend there is TV, drink
a glass of milk */ not there /* sitting on a little table?
How to explain the poems we write incessantly
in the corner of the room, backed up against */ imaginary /*
walls that keep us folded in place, the embrace
of a few strewn pillows, the */ unfurnished /* blanket we pull
over shoulders hunched against the backside
of yet another chair, the toys, the thrown toys; you there,
me here—*he / she / they* reenacting memories, and the way
there are not pillows or blankets or diversions
enough, nor contextualization */ hours of light /*?

At a Monastic Retreat

Pop of a water heater, crackle of beams,
    my small cabin sputtering,
the only machine in a landscape—
    one startled emotion into the next
calling the forest to attention,
    imaginations thriving in the otherwise
silence. Last night, I had to explain
    the wintering habits of nailed-down
wood and how most things were not meant
    to be constrained in one place—
my daughter calling, afraid,
    as her father's house made similar sounds,
brilliant ghosts of cut pine fattening
    the noiseless night, and all her limbic
energy panicking. It's quiet here too,
    I say, *otherworldly* quiet—
desirable *and* unnerving. A large
    picture window voyeurs three sleek deer
against impressionist white, the landscape
    blossoming with snow this early Tuesday
morning as I hug a hot mug of coffee
    close to my chest, a distant stab
of sound swallowing their bodies in deep
    timber gray. *Do this*, I tell my daughter
hunkered against her father's empty corner recliner:
    pull three tubes of paint
from your artist's satchel, add water and brushes,
    then canvas—now enter its blankness, wildly.

The Hunter

—of the man that shot O-Six

Perhaps if he could have touched, while living,
the soft coat, white and gray, full around her face,
and listened for hours to her breathing [not
that you could get that close].

Or observed the tenderness with which she licked and groomed
her shyest pup as he playfully curled into a ball
she had to unknot to clean him. Perhaps
if he had made a bed near her den and slept all night

like a watchdog guarding a litter of lives as the moon
rose high and the forest stirred and swayed with subtleties
that one should be afraid of. Maybe,
if he had grown hungry at the same points in a day she

and her pups were hungry without fulfillment of their needs
for hours—maybe then, he would pray
they all found something to eat. Prayer
might even be a ritual learned quickly if he tracked

in their tracks, met their rivals, fought their wars, understood
that the valley was full of potential enemies.
And when her companions lay down to die from wounds,
possibly this would be the moment a sharp pain beat inside

his chest, seeing now, her eyes. I often wonder
if the men who harassed me after my divorce would recoil
any desire for me born of ambition, ego, and lust
if they knew the countless days I spent holding my son

as he asked me the hard questions about his father:
*Why is he so angry? What did I do wrong? Mom, why isn't Dad
proud of me?* And I stroked his hair,
my breath hot against my own hand. And I rocked him.

And our stomachs growled together—hour
by hour—long into the evening before his father came home.

The Book of Birds

My son studies the Book of Birds,
a pair of binoculars slung over
his slim frame,

        learning

wingspan (short, long), tail
(tufted, straight), bodies (speckled, spotted,
vivid, dull).

        Singing

their sound (whistle, whirl, whimper, coo,
chip note, call note, caw),

        his arms falling open
beneath the book's cover and spine,

eyes working through
the Latin names—

a hungry hatchling looking the part
of *Tringa semipalmata,*
beak pressed into

a freshwater fog,
gold hair feathered over an ear then
curved along his jawline, merging
with his throat.

        He moves
into the marsh grass and mist,
        adapting its sinew and strength.

After My Father Tells Me He Loves the 23rd Psalm

I consider the list of things I've held against him,
circling my finger around the ridge of a glass I don't drink from.
Your mother is in the hospital again, he says; he's signing
the papers for "no resuscitation."

I listen to him cry over the phone about the woman who,
for years, he complained never took his advice.
And of course, I think of all the times
he never took advice. The world is full of hypocrites. I know;

I keep telling myself I have no religion, but really,
I do. Mom, I say, will go *home*, as though it's the most beautiful gift
he could give: to let her.
I want to shepherd him kindly, even if an afterlife proves to be

an illusion, not also admitting I need to believe
there's a place my mother will go.
My father weeps softly over the phone, gently prodding offenses
away—leading me in paths of righteousness.

Field Note on Gaston Bachelard's *The Poetics of Space*

The wildflower book says the petals
    of *Achillea millefolium*
can be crushed to powder and applied
    to wounds to stop bleeding.
A patch of dormant yarrow lives and waits
    for winter's passing
to the west of my cabin.
    The Navajos called it *life's medicine*.
Bullet wounds. Shrapnel wounds.
    December chill. Barren trees
hug the hill behind and do not shade
    my space from the bright afternoon
sun. My desk faces south
    below a window framing the lake
as I flip through the pages of the book
    then set it aside to begin arranging
my things as though I am home—
    though not. My hands
find first the bag of my mother's ashes.
    To stop the bleeding, I set the velvet bag
next to the book, hear dogs barking
    from the cabin nearby,
piercing the stolid silence in these Appalachian
    foothills, pray
because I need to, no other reason,
    [wounds don't heal; they age],
crush the words inside my mouth
    so I can taste the things they name.
I've spoken them before;
    now she can hear me.
Bullet wound. Shrapnel wound.
    December chill, the barren trees.

My Grandmother's Ashes

are somewhere, earth-born, and not ashes at all. Bone and sand
that scatter and remain. Particles
of time always filtering through, whetted, reshaped—always
excavatable. I kept the phone close and listened
to my cousin's voice as Grandmother was dying, reading
Psalm 46—*we will not fear though the earth give way*—one
by one laying shell fragments I recently collected
from a shoreline atop the soil enclosing roots of plants growing
all over my home,
each thumb of new green that sprouts up, witness. *Though its waters
foam and roar*, she continues, stems and leaves reaching
for a bright spot of sun. *Though the mountains tremble
at its swelling*, my cousin drifts silent, her breath shallow as I sit
on the floor cradling a handful of shells,
rocking—in the future she will be mineral, calcium, phosphorus.

EDITH MAY
(CAMP)
BEDFORD
(1926–2008)

The World Is Whatever We Choose to Make It

My daughter stares out at the horizon through a camera picturing
she and I in a midwestern landscape, flaming

pink blush of sunset against coarse cornstalks turned dark charcoal
for the eye to imagine the fields will never appear

any other way than the way she has seen them. *The world
is whatever we choose to make it*, she writes below the photograph

on Instagram, then turns the camera outward again,
this time to say *live however you want*, and posts our elongated shadows

against the sidewalk in this small town where we spend a Saturday.
Yesterday, the trees were flocked with bronze and burnt-orange hues,

but today they begin to shed their leaves, and she asks us to *decide
what to do with the time that is given us.*

We round the corner of a street to see Lake Michigan—
in her feed she calls it *the ocean*. We both want to live

by the ocean someday. But maybe, as she says,
we are already here: the shoreline, the breakers, the seashells we take.

Elegy for My Daughter Who Has Never Known a Paradise

She is dark coat and seed, blonde shock into the wind, the earth
rounding a bend of sand to greet her, lift a grassy spray,

splash up, always vanishing in her media feed by plastic or acid
or use of fossil fuels—the impending end to her not-yet

beginning. Yesterday, Atlantic; today, the Salish Sea.
What whale will consume her compassion? What plot of milkweed

will she harvest and weed? Even I attend the funeral of a stranger
in Mexico—his body discovered carved up among trees—

while my daughter spots koalas burning in Australia,
asks me to *hurry* and *see*. We listen as a woman bursts from the bushes

shirtless, one singed mammal wrapped up in her tee, the phone
poised between our faces and the Great Lake before us,

cold waves pounding over its well-deserted beach. Should I tell her
this shoreline is also eroding, the sand dune sliding away

beneath her guileless feet? We have long known that zebra clams
are bothering these waters, but of *Brachionus leydigii* and *Thermocyclops*

crassus little is known. Ecologists say they might harmlessly adapt
to the climate of Lake Erie—they also predict they may not.

Civil Assault

My stalker has sent
another message
via another Messenger account
that I do not recognize,
listing all the things he'd like to do
to my body.

A policewoman reads the message, dismissing it
due to overuse of the word *sweet*.
He would like to tongue
my *sweet* vagina.
He would like to look deep into
my *sweet* and beautiful eyes.
He would like to be
sweet to me all the time,
have me as his *sweet*
and loving wife.

I understand—I teach
written composition at a local university
and know adjectives
are good indications of intention;
my students should use them sparingly.

As does the policewoman when she says
they won't be able to find my stalker's
exact location
after I show her he says he can find me,
then names my city.
Ah, she answers,
this is when we'll find him
(when he finds me).

I discover his location
an hour after she leaves me, decide
not to burden the system with this information.
A considerate instructor,
I opt not to give the policewoman
more paperwork to write.

This Much

Each year, monarchs re-populate in the Corn Belt, that vast
agricultural region in America's heartland where they lay their eggs
on milkweed plants in spring while migrating north to Canada.

My friend Cruz and I stand in what used to be a cornfield,
now his handiwork of garden plots for immigrant families
and milkweed plants to provide a landing pad

for sojourning monarchs to lay their eggs. Here, they reproduce,
and the caterpillars are sometimes whisked into jars
and kept in homes, then freed after incubation to ensure that yet

another butterfly survives the season despite their overall
declining numbers worldwide. I hold my own jar
frocked with milkweed stem as Cruz tells me how long

until the caterpillar will incubate and how long incubation
will be. But once home, the caterpillar eats and eats its way
up the stem in the jar then dies there, a long white string

extending from its body. My daughter says that this string
is a sign of a pre-existing parasite. *Not your fault Mom*, she says,
starring into her computer where she reads all about

monarch diseases and death. Still, that gnawing sensation
that I failed a whole species by not saving this one, not knowing
what could have been done to cure it of the tiny predator

under its flesh. Peering into the glass jar, insect shriveled
and dangling, I am reminded that, years ago, my family
witnessed my shaken mind as the memories of abuse and assault

came rushing back and, like a tiny predator,
traveled through my psyche, feasting on the tissue of my present
and future with terrors from my past. They watched

but could do nothing to save me from this unraveling and,
in their own fear of exposure as helpless and vulnerable gods,
accused me then and there of dying, then turned away—

as I began, alone, working out my narratives,
hoping they would appreciate my trying. The caterpillar
hung in the jar for a whole two weeks before I decided to clean it out

as I let our mutual helplessness exist between us, refusing to ignore
its obvious shame. *Love is never a failure*, a friend of mine tells me,
and I know he means to add, *even if it's lost*. I caress

the side of the jar consoling myself concerning this dead would-be
monarch, its tiny fingerlike worm sutured to the lid,
knowing how long and hard it fought to accomplish just this much.

Root

Vinegar and spit, a slit of broken breath,
    the vein coiled as noose,
finger-depth, tugging to keep itself
    rooted;
stalk grown into bone,
    muscle, tooth, digested particles
of food, green waste—all that is left
    of a dialect, an agony wounded
with tongue, its flesh winnowed
    by table knife
splitting skin, circling rot,
    letting it bleed without tourniquet;
but to pull it,
    to drag its agony out of the earth,
to temper with its permanence:
    how will the body subsist?
Remove your hand,
    let it linger, ruminate the waste,
soft inside the muscle,
    bruised among the veins—it is all
that is left of a memory,
    saliva mixed up with what's chewed;
how if you try to sort the particles,
    you will see that they are braided,
threads of indivisible need;
    how the body goes limp without
its history;
    how the root supports
the barley, the clover, the weed.

They Tell Us to Live in the Moment
Because the Moment Is All We May Have

Coos Canyon forms a natural pool, shallow at points,
deep at others. Local Mainers come here on hot days to cool off.
My bikini is in the car, but we have stopped here for only a moment
to feel the water slide through the smooth rocks and our toes
as my guide takes photo after photo of me sitting on a dry surface
between currants, telling me to be careful not to slip.

I tell him I am careful just before I nearly slip.
He eyes me, smiling, already getting how I am. The sun
is feverish this August afternoon, and we have just hiked down
a mountain. I want to soak my whole body in the pool
like the other swimmers taking advantage of this perfect summer day,
each mellow vortex swirling between my toes and around the rocks,

begging me to enter their dervish. The water feels sanguine
in its time pushing back at any thought for tomorrow
or the next day or the day after that. My guide steps lightly
over flat rocks as the canyon swallows the current beyond
and beneath us then carries it away. *I need to get back*, I say. Michigan.
The water gurgles in reply as he fidgets with his phone,

high noon reflecting off its surface and falling all around us
like confused snow, the pools shimmering up. *Will I ever
hear from you again?* he asks, walking beside me toward the parking lot,
leaving the question behind. We drive the pined road
away from the canyon, longer for its silence: no plan,
no pause, no projected ambitions—no language for phrasing *goodbye*.

Smile Back

Tiny oyster shells
shift among the orange pebbles
and dirt
along Shoal Creek. I don't
expect to find shells here
in Joplin,
gather their thin chalk bodies
into my pocket.
Traffic noise reverberates
against graffitied rock walls
that line the opposite side of the creek
as my sandaled feet
shift in dry loose sediment
and a bright yellow face
smiles at me
behind pink dogwood blooms,
its paint seemingly fresh—or freshened.
I smile back, inhuman
though it be. Still,
to smile back is something
to practice and repeat
over and over again.
I wave at its sprayed-on expression.
The creek rushes between us.
The traffic rushes beyond us.
The shells inside my pocket
churn softly against my hip—*click*
click click.

Acknowledgments

Thank you to the following magazines and journals for first publishing poems from this book:

About Place Journal: "A Patch of Blue"; "This Much"; "The World Is Whatever We Choose to Make It"

Adanna Literary Magazine: "The Hunter"; "Unpacking"

The Comstock Review: "Elegy for Charley"; "On the Ishnala Trail"

The Free State Review: "My Mother Wears a Bikini at South Haven Beach"

Harbor Review: "Upon Viewing Katrín Sigurdardóttir's *Metamorphic*"

The Headlight Review: "Old Shell"; "The Unusual Art of Living Well"

HIVES Buzz-zine: "First Visit to the Sister Survivors Exhibit"

The Laurel Review: "After I Tell a Man I Can't Date Him Because of My Hidden Disability"

Lunch Ticket: "They Tell Us to Live in the Moment Because the Moment Is All We May Have"

The Maine Review: "A Pedagogy for Lesser Bodies"

The MockingHeart Review: "Root"

Mom Egg Review: "How to Forgive the Predator"

The Night Heron Barks: "At the Eli and Edythe Broad Art Museum"

North Dakota Quarterly: "The Howl"; "My Daughter and I Gather Stones at Empire Beach"

The Other Journal: "After Leaving"

Rust + Moth: "After My Father Tells Me He Loves the 23rd Psalm"

Salamander Magazine: "Elegy for My Daughter Who Has Never Known a Paradise"; "I Wanted to Be a Boy"

Split Rock Review: "Field Note on Gaston Bachelard's *The Poetics of Space*" (III); "Steven Turnball"

Terrain.org: "The Book of Birds"

Welter: "Civil Assault"

West Trade Review: "Field Note on Gaston Bachelard's *The Poetics of Space*" (II)

"At a Monastic Retreat," "Elegy for My Daughter Who Has Never Known a Paradise," "My Grandmother's Ashes," "Spirit of the Animal," and "The

World Is Whatever We Choose to Make It" were published in *Aeolian Harp Series Anthology of Poetry Folios* (Glass Lyre Press, 2021).

"At the Butterfly Habitat" and "Protections" were published in Crystal S. Gibbins, ed., *Rewilding: Poems for the Environment* (Flexible Press, 2020).

"Protections" was published in Sean Prentiss and Joe Wilkins, *Environmental and Nature Writing: A Writer's Guide and Anthology*, 2nd ed. (Bloomsbury Academic, Bloomsbury Publishing, 2025).

Thank you to Michigan State University for granting me employment that rescued me from homelessness and to my friend Matt Rossi for helping me make that connection. Most importantly, a hearty thanks to Dennis Hinrichsen, the first poet laureate of Lansing, Michigan, for being a supportive friend and helping me hone these poems and manuscript. Thank you also to Cruz Villarreal for inviting me to weed the milkweed garden for monarchs. Had a global pandemic not changed my plans, I would have spent more time there.

Monson Arts in Maine and Owsley Forks in Kentucky gave me writing residencies while I worked on these poems. My gratitude to both. I am especially grateful for the generosity and kindness of Lynda and Coleman at Owsley. It was a treasure to spend a whole month in the late bell hooks's cabin as I wrote these poems even as she passed into eternity in the neighboring town of Berea while I was there, merely a couple of months after my mother had passed. Thank you for the space to grieve my loss and your companionship during the holiday season so I wouldn't be alone.

And God bless my children for surviving this rending with me. They have been constantly supportive and open through it all. Dailey and Ryley, being your mother is an honor and a joy, and I pray our futures will close all gaps in our histories.

Gratitude for the grandmothers I barely knew. I carry you both.

And, finally, to my mother in whatever eternity there is: I praise you. You were a fire, a force, a cool rain, a gracious breeze on my face through every harsh season. You live forever in me.

Notes

Selections about O-Six and the rewilding of wolves to Yellowstone National Park were based on readings from the book *American Wolf: A True Story of Survival and Obsession in the West* by Nate Blakeslee. Her story is referenced in the following poems: "The Howl," "Steven Turnball," "Protections," and "The Hunter." "My Daughter and I Gather Stones at Empire Beach" also refers to other wolves that were rewilded in Yellowstone and mentioned in the book.

O-Six was born in 2006 in the Apple Creek Pack in Yellowstone, and she established the Lamar Valley Pack as a three-year-old in the Lamar River Valley from 2010 to 2012. This valley was easily accessible, allowing researchers and tourists to observe the pack. Steven Turnball is not the actual name of the hunter that shot O-Six in 2012; rather, it is the alias created by Nate Blakeslee to shield the hunter's identity. According to Blakeslee, O-Six was shot at close range, "more or less" in someone's front yard.

Lines in "Gestation" are from Pablo Neruda's poem "The Word" as translated by Stephan Mitchell in *Full Woman, Fleshly Apple, Hot Moon* (Harper Perennial Modern Classics, 1997).

Gaston Bachelard excerpts are from *The Poetics of Space* (Beacon Press, 1969).

E. W. Bäärnhielm excerpt is from "Song of the Seashell" found in the essay "Seashell Sound" by Stefan Helmreich published in *Cabinet Magazine*, no. 48 (Winter 2012–13).

Several books on trauma were read and contributed to producing poems in this collection. Notably, these books include *The Body Keeps the Score: Brain, Mind, and Body in Healing Trauma* by Bessel van der Kolk and *It Didn't Start with You: How Inherited Trauma Shapes Who We Are and How to End the Cycle* by Mark Wolynn.

Additional information on shell symbolism can be found in Dr. Rex Van Vuuren, "Much in a Little: Reflections on the Gift of a Sea-Shell," *Indo-Pacific*

Journal of Phenomenology 3, no. 1 (November 2003) and Stefan Helmreich, "Seashell Sound," *Cabinet Magazine*, no. 48 (Winter 2012–13).

The Ishnala Trail, featured in the poem with that name, is in Mirror Lake State Park, Wisconsin.

My mother died early morning October 27, 2021, in Texas.

BACKWATERS PRIZE IN POETRY

The Backwaters Prize in Poetry was suspended from 2005 to 2011.

To order or obtain more information on these or other University of Nebraska Press titles, visit nebraskapress.unl.edu.

2 04

9 781496 243706